FEARFULLY
STRONG

FEARFULLY
STRONG

BREAKING THROUGH THE
TERROR BARRIER

PAULA JEAN FERRI

Fearfully Strong
Breaking Through the Terror Barrier
Text Copyright © 2020 by Paula Jean Ferri

paulajeanferri.com

Cover Design by Megan Sawyer Buck of Pixel Perfect
Interior book design by Francine Platt, Eden Graphics, Inc.

ISBN 978-0-9997673-1-3

1. Main Category Non-Fiction—Self-Help
2. Sub Category Non-Fiction—Communication and Social Skills
3. Sub Category Non-Fiction— Motivational and Inspirational

First Edition
10 9 8 7 6 5 4 3 2 1
Printed in the United States of America

Dedicated to Travis "Trigger" Smith
who claimed he couldn't read so he could do
stupid shit anyways. Thanks for being fearless
and taking care of your scaredy-cat sister.

TABLE OF CONTENTS

INTRODUCTION

Cody PULLED ME closer to the ledge. "Look at that view!" It was indeed stunning, at least the pictures show it that way. I managed to be a little too busy being grateful for the guard rail. The dizzying height made me clutch it even tighter. Soon my knuckles were white, but I couldn't stop the spinning. My stomach dropped each time I tried to look anywhere but at my hands. The lush green landscape melting into the Pacific Ocean wasn't quite enough for me not to notice the sharp drop directly in front of me.

I heard Cody's voice ask me, "Are you ok?"

"Of course!" I lied as I took a few steps back. My head stopped spinning and my stomach returned to its rightful place. How could I not be ok? I was living in Hawaii, loving my college classes, surrounded by great people and life was just about perfect. As long as I stayed away from the many cliffs and ledges on the island. Or at least didn't look down.

I am afraid of heights. As in terrified. While I know the views are phenomenal without any obstructions, I like them a few feet back and enjoy seeing the guard rail in my line of sight. I like having my stomach stay put and not feeling dizzy enough to fall over the rail plummeting to my death.

The problem is that I knew I wouldn't be living in Hawaii forever. I would not always be able to enjoy the beauty that I lived in. I would have loved to come just a little closer to the edge to get the full effect of the view over the Hawaiian landscape. And looking back, I wish I hadn't left that day without seeing the full view.

We all have things we are afraid of. Fear is a very common emotion, if not the most common. Some have more than their fair share, while others seem to be completely fearless. Yet even the fearless have moments that shake them to the core. Everyone knows what it's like to be afraid. Not everyone knows what to do about it or how to use it.

This book will address fear in three ways: benefits of facing fear, as well as identifying different types of fears, and how to move past them. Almost everything we want is on the other side of fear. Promotions, career changes, love, fulfillment, purpose and success to name just a few. All require us to step outside of our comfort zone and take some sort of risk, which often incites fear.

It will be terrifying, it may be awkward or painful, too. However, for every action, there is an equal and opposite reaction*. This may be a science principle discovered by Sir Isaac Newton, but the principle applies in other areas as well. Unless you want to be living your life in neutral, watching life pass you by, you will have to face hard and scary things in order to get the good stuff. Once you get to the good stuff, it all seems worth it and you may even find yourself wanting to do it again.

The purpose of this book is to take a close look at our fears. More particularly at the fears that are holding us back from living our best and most fulfilling lives. Those fears that put us between a rock and a hard place and in those times when we want to move forward, but are too afraid. The only other option allows the fear to win out, giving it more strength the next time around.

As human beings, the abilities we have are incredible. We are intelligent creatures with the ability to make choices. We have these brains that are able to think and process rather than passively respond to what happens around us. We have the benefit—and responsibility—to use the brains we have been given. With knowledge we can overcome those fears. As this quote from L. Frank Baum's *The Wonderful Wizard of Oz* says, "A baby has brains, but it doesn't know much. Experience is the only thing that brings knowledge, and the longer you are on earth the more experience you are sure to get."

If we come to a place where fear arises and we instantly back down, deciding we don't really want the thing after all, because it isn't worth the fear. What does that leave us with? Not much. Life's leftovers are the lowest paying jobs, the relationships others don't want and a life full of negativity, complaining, thinking we aren't worth it, etc. Life heads into a downward spiral. I don't want life's leftovers. I don't want fear to rule my life. I'm taking back my life by taking control and ownership. I'm going to use the knowledge and experience I have. If you take the time to join me, you will find you can do the same.

*Newton's Third Law of Motion, *Principia Mathematica Philosophiae Naturalis*. 1686

DEFINITION OF COURAGE

What is Fear? What is Courage?

THE OXFORD DICTIONARY defines fear as "an unpleasant emotion caused by the belief that someone or something is dangerous, likely to cause pain, or a threat, the likelihood of something unwelcome happening, a mixed feeling of dread and reverence." This definition covers just about everything, doesn't it? The definition of fear covers danger, pain, dread, unwanted or unwelcome changes and even reverence—or being in awe of someone or something. The last is not one we will really look at though. I want to focus on the fear that holds us back more than awe.

Based on the definition, no wonder fear is so common. That just sounds like so many experiences we have from day to day. Life can be pretty painful or even dangerous. Some situations are certainly unwanted and dreaded.

Let's take a look at the inverse. Courage is defined in the Oxford dictionary as "the ability to do something that frightens one; strength in the face of pain or grief." Which is NOT fearlessness—or not being afraid at all. Courage is being afraid and doing it anyways. By this standard, there are far more courageous people than there are fearless people. If there are so many courageous people, who is to say that we can't be one of them?

In day to day life, we encounter fear often. Author Candyce Ossefort-Russell has described two types of fear, which she calls danger-fear and challenge-fear in her article on Medium "2 Mistakes You Make Because You're Scared, and How to Avoid Them." Danger-fear is our bodies' natural response to fight, flee or freeze in the face of physical danger. On the other hand, challenge-fear is when your body is facing new and unknown experiences. They can be closely related. Sometimes new experiences can put us in physical danger, like the first time you go skydiving. This can potentially be physically dangerous, but it is also a new experience to you—and to me if I ever decide to do it. Fear of heights, remember? But let's say I wanted to try. I'm obviously going to be terrified. Why? Because it's dangerous or because it's new? I'll be honest, it's likely due to the newness of the activity that scares me the most. Many others have been skydiving and there are precautions made and equipment to keep me safe. According to the United States Parachute Association, I would have to jump 100,000 times before I would push my luck and experience some kind of equipment malfunction that would actually end in death. So this isn't a logical fear, or really much of a danger-fear. Probability says I'm more likely to die in a car accident. I drive every day and without fear. So logically, that makes skydiving more of a challenge-fear. It's something new and unknown and is a challenge our bodies are simply trying to prepare for.

That doesn't change the fact that the fear is present. And very, very real. It does help, however, to narrow down what we are really afraid of and how we respond to this fear. Despite the fact that skydiving may seem death defying, it isn't the only thing that we are really afraid of. A deeper cause might be that we don't trust the equipment, we don't trust the instructor (we barely know them, after all), or we don't trust our own luck (of *course* I'd be the one in 100,000 with the faulty equipment that's going to snap and I'm going to die).

Any of these underlying fears can be addressed and, with time, potentially overcome. However, the faster and more direct route, rather than waiting until a fear is overcome to dive in, is to simply do it. That is where courage comes in. Remember, courage is not the absence of fear, it's doing the thing despite the presence of fear.

Nike: The Origins

Most people don't realize where the famous athletic company got the name. One origin was the Greek goddess Nike, goddess of victory, but there is also an ancient Greek legend during a time of war with Persia that involves the name. After the Battle of Marathon, Athenian runner Pheidippides was sent to announce the victory to the rulers of Athens. He ran the 25 miles from the battlefield to Athens, proclaimed victory (in Greek Niki), then died of exhaustion.*

What does this have to do with fear? It connects, I promise. Let's think about what went through his mind. Do you think before dying of exhaustion, he might have felt tired? Why didn't he stop? Just two minutes to catch his breath wouldn't hurt right? I mean, his life was literally at risk. So this could go one of two ways. Either he was terrified of whatever punishment would await for not doing his job as quickly as possible, or he legitimately was so overcome with joy (as the stories say) that he didn't fear what would come as a result of running so hard and so fast.

Either way, we can learn a lesson. We can either feel another emotion so strongly that the fear disappears completely—or at least enough to move forward (it can go either way)—or the fear can motivate us. This is certainly something to consider when looking at fear. It does motivate us to move beyond where we currently are and allow us to perform great feats of strength. If you are job hunting and you fear where you will live and how you will eat, you are suddenly much more motivated to put in five job applications a day rather than five per week. If you are running away from a lion, you will be running a lot faster than if you were simply running in a 100 meter dash in a school race.

Fear affects us physically, it's not just an emotional state. It is a mechanism that has always been used for survival. In today's world, that definition of survival has changed dramatically, and so has our view of fear. In today's society, we now fear anything from killer clowns to talking with people. This is a fairly new phenomenon. Little things that used to make people anxious, uncomfortable or nervous have progressed to fully developed and paralyzing fears.

However, we can still use that fear and the physiological response within our bodies to move forward. Fear changes hormone levels, produces adrenaline and initiates one of three responses to the danger: fight, flight or freeze. Fear enhances our ability to achieve any one of these successfully, and depending on the particular fear we face, what our initial reaction is to challenges.

Did you know that your response to fear is actually very telling? For example, in nature, the animals most likely to freeze in a dangerous situation are usually those that are preyed upon. The good news is that this is not an idea set in stone and can be changed. Just because I have a habit of freezing when I am afraid, doesn't mean that will always be the case. I want to be the type of person who is able to take charge of a scary situation and move through it, saying, "Yeah, I did that."

This book contains the things I have learned as I willingly put myself in situations that scare me. I'm tired of being afraid. I'm sick of freezing and afterwards wishing the outcome had been different. So I'm changing and evolving. The growth I have experienced is unparalleled. I have learned more in the past six months than I have in the past six years.

In August of 2017, I quit my full time job to spend my time writing, studying and publishing my second book. This was a huge risk. I had been thinking about doing it for months. I had told this idea to several family members and friends who all discouraged the idea. The more I talked about it, the more they scared me. There were so many things to consider. However, I did it despite the encouragement of fear from those I trust most.

As terrifying as it was for me and for those around me, this was one of the best things I have ever done for myself. Sure, the rough stuff happened. I spent more than I brought in from book sales, there were a few missed payments and I financially set myself back, but the learning experiences I had and the person I became in those six months were invaluable. Yes, it lasted only six months and I have a full time job again. But if I had the chance to do it again with a greater focus on financial responsibility, I would do it in a heartbeat.

There are other things that are more important to me than focusing on the fear itself. Take a lesson from history and push beyond fear to reach your destination. You have great things coming.

*Other stories state he ran about 150 miles in two days, adding to the exhaustion and making the tale more believable, though the tale is still unaccounted for in its veritability.

Sacrifice/Priorities

It doesn't matter what the motivation for Pheidippides was. It might have been another fear, it might have been some noble cause. We will never know. That doesn't mean that there isn't a lesson to be learned from this story. There was something stronger than his fear of death. Which, let's be honest, is a pretty large fear for most people.

So assuming Pheidippides was afraid of death like most human beings, there would have been a very strong motivation that was more important than this fear. If we want to be able to overcome any fear, we have to realize that there will be something more important than this temporary emotion.

For example, I am afraid of heights. However, if my nephews climbed somewhere they shouldn't be and slipped, you can bet I would be up there after them. My nephews are more important to me than my fear. While my nephews may be a bit reckless, this is not a situation I have to deal with every day.

That's another thing about fear. A lot of the worst case scenarios we picture in our minds, really aren't everyday situations anyways. So many of our fears are based off of the most terrible thing that can happen. We play these scenarios in our minds and they aren't realistic in any way. While possible for a meteor to hit the earth, it isn't likely to happen anytime soon. What are the odds—the literal statistics—of you being in a plane crash, or eaten by a shark or bitten by a snake? It doesn't matter what the fear is, statistically, it just isn't likely.

So why do we allow ourselves to stress over such things? We try to prepare for these large catastrophes that might happen, like a zombie apocalypse, but we can't quite seem to give that presentation at work. Both terrifying situations. One might be a little more likely to happen and should be a bit more of a priority as far as preparation.

Other times, we let the little things scare us just because we don't want to do them. We stress over the work it takes to prepare, then stress over not being prepared. Sometimes we go the other direction and over prepare, yet are still terrified, but that is for another section. Let's focus on the former right now, shall we?

Whether you are scared and don't prepare or don't prepare then become scared, that fear is getting in your way. One of the most tragic things I see (and see often) is how people give in to the fear, rather than making what they care about the main focus and priority. A work presentation can be terrifying. Speaking in front of people just isn't most people's idea of a good time. It certainly isn't mine.

However, I have an important message I want to say, and that is more important to me than my fear and self-comfort. This work presentation is more important than your fear. Fear is temporary and presenting is part of your life. If you do it once at work, chances are good you will have to do it again and again.

Your job is more important than your fear. And if it isn't, find a new job. This can also be terrifying, to leave a place where you have security. So which fear are you willing to face more often? The fear of presenting or the fear of finding a new job? There can be fear in literally everything that we do, but we have to determine what is more important than our fear.

Coming back to the presentation idea, the good news is you won't die during a presentation, at least not because of the presentation itself. The fear of it may cause a heart attack, but that's what this book is for, right? Sure, it might be awkward. Worst case scenario is something embarrassing can happen. You can recover from that. That won't matter tomorrow, or even next week. Another bit of good news, you get to have a new experience, learn from it and be better at it next time. If your priorities are in the right place, you can move forward despite fear. And if you do it again and again, you start to realize the fear isn't there anymore.

What's the worst that could happen? You've probably already done it. The best that could happen? You might have already done that, too. Most presentations will fall in the muddy middle. They aren't really traumatizing, but still leave room for work and improvement. As time goes on and this muddy middle grows, you become desensitized to the fear that used to prevail before the first few presentations.

As we focus on what is most important to us, we have to make sacrifices. We have to be willing to give up what is less important. Is your fear more important than the goal you have set or experience you want to have? What is most important to you and the life you want to live?

Just do it

Sometimes all we really need is just five seconds of not thinking. A lot of fear is based on our predisposed thoughts of the worst things that could possibly happen. If we simply stop thinking and do the thing, we can pass over that barrier that is standing in our way. Just like standing on the edge of a swimming pool, wanting to jump in. We know it's going to be cold, and the longer we stand there agonizing over it, the less likely we are to actually jump in. Stop thinking and just jump! Once we get past that initial shock of cold water, our bodies acclimate and we are good to simply enjoy the water.

So it turns out Nike (the shoe company) actually has it right. Their motto, "just do it" is often the best advice. When everything we want is on the other side of this invisible and imaginary wall, why do we not just cross it? Often when I stop and look at the things that terrify me, it's because I've built up some large, dramatic scene. The actual event and change itself is often anticlimactic. I find myself thinking, "that's it?" Then I wonder why I put it off so long in the first place.

Just by way of example, I have another story for you. Graduating high school was terrifying for me. I had known nothing outside of my small little town and had gone to school with the same people since kindergarten. I didn't want to leave them. It was familiar and comfortable. Yet not once did the flow of time stop, as much as I wished it would. I kept going about my days: going to class, doing homework (kinda, I mean, senioritis played a role too), doing chores at home and spending time with my friends. Graduation came and went, and while classes stopped, I didn't feel any different. It was painless and I felt a little let down in a way. Wasn't this supposed to be some life-changing event where I suddenly knew all the answers and how to act like a grown up?

The real struggle came when everything was packed in my car and ready for me to simply drive away from home to start college. It probably took longer than it should have. Turns out, I wasn't scared of graduation, so all the stress and worry about the ceremony was pointless. This however, was a bit more painful. And all it was going to take was simply starting the car I had driven for the past year. This moment was the one I had really feared, so I put it off. I dawdled, taking my time to double and triple check that I had everything.

I couldn't even say multiple goodbyes, because my parents were both gone to work.

Life goes on, their lives weren't on the precipice of change quite like mine was—though they did have to face the change of not having me around—they weren't moving, they still had jobs to go to and they still had children to take care of. In my parents' defense, before you gawk at them for not taking time off from work to take me to school, it was only a six hour drive and I was staying with my mom's best friend for a week before I could move into my apartment and classes started. Doing this on my own, while terrifying, was one of the best things they could have done for me.

Going back to the driveway—knowing I was about to start doing everything on my own and that my life would change when I started that car—I wish I had been looking forward instead of looking back. The fear came from letting go of the familiar. I wish I had been more hopeful about the future. If I had any idea of how much more I would have loved college and the new friends I would make, the fascinating things I would learn and the opportunities I had to continue forward with my life, it wouldn't have taken me so long to turn that key. It only took five seconds to start the car. So why did I drag it out for so long?

I had done the same thing throughout most of my life growing up. I always managed to prolong the pain of the inevitable. I remember trying to slowly pry a band-aid away from my skin before my mother came and just yanked it off. It happened so quickly and I was so shocked that my mom would do such a thing, that I didn't even feel any pain. I sure had the pain while slowly trying to pry it away, though. Just like ripping off a band-aid, most transitional moments just need five seconds—or less—of just doing it.

In case you needed one more example, while I was living in Hawaii, my friends and I hiked to several waterfalls. On occasion, the falls we went to were also a perfect jumping point into the clear pools of water below for a refreshing swim. The hike to one particular falls had taken several hours and we were hot and sweaty, even with the stunning views of this hidden gem in paradise. Arriving at the falls, we all quickly jumped in the water to cool off before we started the short climb behind the falls to jump in.

Now, you can't just live in Hawaii and pass up opportunities like this. It was almost like a rite of passage, there are just certain places you have to jump if you live in Hawaii, especially with the daredevil friends I had. Trust me, there were several times I didn't jump, but this one was completely safe and was only about an eight foot drop. It was enough to terrify me though. I wanted to jump and climbed to the top, but that fear of heights got to me again. As I stood there watching my friends jump, then run up and jump again, I knew it wasn't an actual danger that had me afraid. Though the building pressure from my friends was not helping the situation. They were trying to be helpful, but it wasn't quite working for me the way they were hoping it would. It just stressed me out more. I don't remember how long I stood at the top of the falls, swatting at the bugs as I slowly dripped dry.

What I do remember was just getting to a point where I was just so frustrated. I was frustrated with myself for being such a chicken. I was frustrated with my friends that were helping in the wrong way. So while everyone had turned their attention away from me, whether out of boredom, distraction or whatever reason, I saw a small window, stopped thinking and jumped. It took me less than two seconds.

I had a lot of friends try to get me to jump a second time, but I was happy with doing it just one time. I had no need to do it again. I did it because I wanted to, not for their viewing pleasure. I had the experience that I wanted. That's the important part. Doing the things that you want to do, not dictated by fear or by the expectations of others.

It is important to note that just because I did it, the fear didn't go away. I'm still scared of heights, and it was an effort any time I wanted to jump off any of the various cliffs and waterfalls in Hawaii. However, it did get easier knowing I just had to take a deep breath, not think about it and jump. So following attempts at jumping did not take the half hour I took the first time. It doesn't take a deep psychoanalysis of your fears, it doesn't take therapy or soul-searching. Sometimes all it takes is that five seconds.

Depending on the fear, yes, sometimes, there will need to be more deep soul-searching before we can move on and do the thing that scares us. Interestingly enough, no matter how much we want to do that thing, we still put off finding out what is wrong and how to move past it. It took me years to figure out why I had such terrible luck dating. Turns out, I was afraid. Terrified.

You can ask just about anyone and they will tell you that dating is hard and that it is awful, but not everyone was terrified of *men* like I was. I didn't even realize that is what was holding me back for many, many years. And when I did recognize that, I didn't do anything about it for several more years. So for all the years I spent lonely, it was my own fault for not being willing to face my fears.

This realization helped me to sit down and figure out exactly what my problem was and why I was so afraid. Turns out I had been letting past experiences from when I was a child affect how I viewed men. My fear kept most men at arm's length. The only ones willing to push past my many walls and barriers were the ones that kept those fears alive and strong. I was really keeping away the good ones that would help me see that not all men fit this stereotype I had created in my head and feared for so long.

So I decided to sit down and stop making myself miserable. Turns out, I had already lived through what I was most afraid of about men. Meaning several things.

First of all, it couldn't get any worse, it's already happened. Not only that, but I survived it. I'm still here and doing well despite the trauma. Plus, since I lived through it, I can now see more clearly warning signs that I need to avoid so that it doesn't happen again. All super important things to realize if I wanted to move forward with my life. So why did I put it off so long again?

If I had just sat down to look at it as soon as I realized there had been a problem, I could have saved myself years of anxiety and misery. So the overall lesson still stands: Just Do It! No matter if it is your five seconds to just do the thing itself or sitting down to face it no matter how long it takes, you will be glad you did.

Epigenetics

One of my new favorite things is epigenetics. It really shows how incredibly powerful we can be if we recognize our power, which makes it just a little bit harder to be afraid so often. The official definition of epigenetics from the Oxford dictionary is, "the study of changes in organisms caused by modification of gene expression rather than alteration of the genetic code itself." Basically, the genes are there, but we choose how they are expressed. This affects not only our mindset, but can affect us physically as well. Fear is powerful enough that it can make us physically ill at the thought of doing something. It can also affect subtle communication cues such as how we stand.

Basically epigenetics is the concept of mind over matter put into scientific terms. As a simplified version, it is the ability of our body to change our biology. We cannot change our basic DNA, the color of your eyes won't change without the assistance of colored contact lenses, but it does mean that we can change things by changing our mindset. We can change from a night owl to a morning person or a variety of other "inherent traits" that we think are just how we are.

Fear falls into this category. We can change our fears and remove them completely if we so desire. This won't happen overnight—and it does take a lot of work—but if a certain fear is holding you back from living the life you want, it becomes all the more rewarding to push forward. Just because that is how things have always been, doesn't mean it is forever written in the stars to be that way.

I spent many years studying as a vocalist, and posture is very important to get the correct sound. However, as I spent less time in the music world and more time hunched over a computer for my day job and for my own writing, my posture has changed and it isn't as good as it used to be. In fact, it was only really good when I was singing. I didn't walk the same way I stood. During this time, I was a very shy and quiet individual. If you asked me a direct question, you would be lucky to hear me speak rather than give a simple nod or head shake. Yet I could sing in front of a large crowd with little to no fear. I changed when I was singing. I changed in part because my posture changed.

I have recently started to focus more on my posture all around, not just as a musician. I keep my chin up— not just figuratively, but parallel to the floor. I keep my shoulders back. Not only does it look better, but I *feel* better. I feel stronger, more confident. The shy person I was growing up is disappearing. I can't really call myself shy the way I used to in high school or even my early college years.

Confidence is created by you. The more this posture becomes second nature, the more that strength becomes second nature as well. Because I physically made a very small change, my personality got a major reboot. This is epigenetics in a nutshell. It can actually go a lot deeper than this, but this is the most pertinent example to this book. Even just the way we stand when we face a fear will make a difference.

It's hard to stand at the edge of a cliff and jump— even when we know it's safe thanks to safety equipment, a large pool of water and the example of friends who are jumping multiple times—if you are afraid of heights. However, if every time that you faced this fear of heights, rather than shrink back, you square your shoulders, lift your chin and take a deep breath, that confidence can take over, even just for a moment. But sometimes a moment is all you really need.

Once this action is repeated time and time again, you start sending signals to your body that you aren't really afraid after all. With time, it can become a more natural process and help you completely overcome a fear of heights. This is key with any fear you may have. Square your shoulders, look it in the eye and just do it.

BENEFITS OF FACING FEARS

WE GET SO CAUGHT UP in our fears that we tend to forget that there are benefits we are missing out on. Not just the benefit of doing the thing we are afraid of, but even the very process of overcoming fear has numerous benefits that just get tossed aside. When we are afraid, that single fear—or even multiple fears—is all-encompassing. They become the only thing in our line of sight. So if we expand that line of sight we are able to see beyond that fear. So take a deep breath, let's look at a few reasons why overcoming fear itself can be a good thing.

Credibility

In overcoming our fears, we gain a sense of admiration from others. Not many people are willing to face their fears. In doing so, there is a sense of respect that has been earned. And who doesn't want a little bit more respect? That respect comes not only from others who admire you for facing your fears, but you can hold your head up a little higher and respect yourself a bit more. You can do and have done hard things! What a confidence booster to know that others now see the hard things you have done despite fear. You get to be a person they admire and a person they want to be like.

It's actually quite weird in my mind to realize that I am that person for other people. I don't feel any different than I did before. I am still afraid of heights. Yet I continue to face that fear and others because I want what is on the other side. Doing the thing that scares you doesn't mean it is going to go away instantly. Sometimes it does. And that is a liberating feeling. Other times, it just hangs around like an old towel you keep forgetting to grab when it's time to do the wash.

However, knowing that you are willing and able to face fears will bring you opportunities. People know they can count on you to get things done. Let's say you have a fear of public speaking. Working to overcome that fear and doing it again and again, even if it scares the daylights out of you every single time, can show a boss that you deserve that promotion that is up for grabs at the office. Your boss knows he can count on you to do things, even when it's terrifying. That effort is hard to find, but when found, is often rewarded.

It's not the fear you are facing that gets that reward, but the simple act of facing the fear, even if it doesn't turn out the way you want it to. Even taking the step toward the fear will separate you from the crowd and give you more credibility than those not willing to even take the first step. The more steps you take, the more you distinguish yourself as someone who does hard things and earn that credibility.

Empathy

Separating and distinguishing yourself has the interesting effect of connecting you with others. You can suddenly relate to more people. Not just those who are afraid, but also those who are trying to overcome their fears. You understand when things don't come out as they hoped or expected. You know what is on the other side and can help. Encouraging others as they become the best version of themselves is one of the best feelings in life.

Everyone struggles with something. It may not even be a fear they are trying to overcome. This idea of doing hard things is so universal though. You know how hard it is. You know what helped you when things were the hardest, the most terrifying, the most bleak. You've been there. You know. That ability to relate to others is invaluable in relationships. Any kind of relationship, whether it be family relationships, romantic ones, friendly ones, business ones, etc. It doesn't matter how you know the person. But the ability to connect with them and relate to them will always help you to understand them in ways you never would have thought of before.

This ability to connect with people will also bring you opportunities you would never have imagined. Sometimes even the act of connecting with others can be hard and terrifying, but the results are again, worth infinitely more than letting the fear hold you back. You just never know where those connections may lead.

Last year, a friend that I went to college with recommended a writing course with Benjamin Hardy. I had no idea who that was. However, this friend, Richie Norton, has an incredible talent for connecting with other people. He is incredibly open with several hard things he has dealt with in his life and times where he was incredibly afraid. He has leveraged those hard times to create his ideal lifestyle and has become someone I admire and want to be like. So I took his advice and joined this course with Ben.

In this course, I was able to have conversations with Ben where it was my turn to be open about things that I struggle with, including my Tourette Syndrome. Because I was willing to share those things, Ben was able to connect me with Richard Paul Evans, an author with Tourette Syndrome. I have known and admired Richard Paul Evans for years as an author, so when Ben produced an opportunity to meet this hero of mine, I was simply elated! I can't even begin to describe how awesome it was to not only meet him, but to connect with him in a way not many others can, and to learn various skills he has honed over the years.

This ability to connect with people provided me with so much that I never could have imagined. I have learned so much from each of these three men and have become so much more capable at living the life I want to live. Each of us had moments where we had to be vulnerable and face our own fears and struggles. However, understanding those hard times and having that empathy and ability to connect has reaped massive benefits in my life. And this isn't something reserved just for me, this comes to anyone willing to take those steps beyond the fears that hold them back.

Problem Solving

Jumping into a fear provides several opportunities for us to think on our feet. If you are like me at all, you have a tendency to freeze when scared, this may seem like a ludicrous idea. Trust me, I get that completely! However, even those with the fight or flee instinct have just one thought that can be expanded into others. That is all the more reason that this kind of "training" is needed. I prefer to look at it as an opportunity to practice doing something I'm terrible at and struggle with.

However, the more I practice this concept in terrifying situations, the easier it is to do in normal situations. And by normal, I mean the stressful moments that we have in our lives from day to day. If I can handle some form of coherent thought while I am looking at a garter snake to remind myself it isn't harmful or poisonous, I can make a decision at work about how to respond when problems arise. The more we use our mental faculties in a fearful situation, the easier and more coherent thought is during everyday situations.

Along the same lines, if we are able to look at something as large as fear in our lives and face it head on, we can conquer anything. For instance, let's use the example of a fear of snakes. I am terrified of them. If I see this as a problem, it gives me a chance to practice how to figure out what exactly the problem is and how to fix it.

Just like with other areas of our lives, we have to first identify the problem before we can break it down into individual parts that can then become stepping stones to help us. We have already identified the problem: fear of snakes. For me, that came from an experience when I was just four years old or so. I grew up in southern Nevada and hearing snakes are dangerous and they can kill you. My family was out for a Sunday drive in the truck—meaning several of us were in the back. My aunt saw a rattlesnake sunning itself and yelled to stop the truck.

While we all stayed in the truck and watched, she teased and played with the snake before chopping off its head, getting rid of the danger. She then threw the body in the back of the truck with us. As we resumed driving, I looked back at where my aunt had tossed the snake and it was moving. Science explains this as the nerves twitching, but a four year old doesn't know this. I was terrified and received a lifelong scar or fear. Even decades later, the things still creep me out.

It's not always possible to identify when the fear started, or to have a logical reason behind the fear. If you can, it can be incredibly helpful in breaking down the problem. Part of the reason it's a problem is because I obviously have a family that isn't afraid of snakes. They play with the dangerous ones and make pets of the non-dangerous ones. I'm going to be around the snakes anyways thanks to my crazy family, so I feel the need to conquer this fear.

Note that blame is not a part of moving past fear. It's not my aunt's fault that I'm afraid of snakes. That came from the snake itself. So looking at the fear, I can logically deduce that a dead snake is dead, even with nerves twitching. I am more afraid of the poisonous bite than the actual snake itself, and as long as I stay out of reach of a poisonous bite from the head, I'm really in no danger. Especially if the snake isn't poisonous.

This means that last year as I was walking up to my apartment and saw a snake, after jumping about three feet into the air, I was able to quickly see this was a simple garter snake. They are not dangerous, and in fact are beneficial to gardens because they eat insects and rodents that would harm the growing plants. Not only that, but it was more scared of me and was moving *away* from me when I saw it and jumped.

Problem solving is a logical process. Utilizing logic in the face of "danger" helped calm my nerves and walk past the snake. My instincts may be yelling, "DANGER!" I then have to counter this by simply yelling back, "FALSE!" I was able to do this for several weeks afterwards as the snake hung around. Using that same method, I can face a problem at work, logically breaking it down and moving past it. These experiences give me greater confidence, knowing I can overcome and solve any problem.

Not only that, but when you have moved past a fear, you have a clear head. Unclouded by fear, you can think much more clearly. This allows you to find more solutions rather than focusing on avoidance of said fear. Either way your brain is going to be thinking of a solution, but the type of solution you come up with from a clear head will have the most impact and better results.

Experience

When I was a little girl I read a lot of books. And by a lot, I mean my parents grounded me from books because they were worried about the lack of balance in my life. Which was incredibly wise of them. Everything I had "experienced" up to this point was through a book. I had zero social experience going into high school which made me more awkward than most. Meaning it was really bad. As I moved into my twenties, I started to see the difference between the knowledge I had obtained from all of these books and the application and use of that knowledge.

There is a stark difference between knowing something and experiencing something. One can read all of the statistics about homelessness, observe the conditions of it and think they know everything there is to know on the subject. But to actually live homeless is a completely different ball park. The amount of homeless individuals in Hawaii is staggering. I saw it all the time, I even knew some people who were homeless and had talked with them and become their friends.

Due to circumstances beyond my control, I was forced to spend a week homeless myself. I had to move out of one apartment by a certain day and wasn't allowed to move into the next until the following week. It was during the summer, so most of my friends had gone home, and I had no other options. This was a game changer for me and a huge eye opener. The lessons I learned during that week based on my experience changed me more than reading about it, or even speaking with people directly, did.

We need to experience things in order to understand them better. Please keep this idea in context and realize that not everything needs to be experienced literally. I have several friends who work as therapists with drug addicts. They do NOT need to go out and do drugs to get the full experience. However, they should understand addiction on a more personal level. This is accomplished by giving up something that is as natural to them as breathing. It could be cutting out sugar from their diet, it could be giving up social media or even not going for a run for an entire week if they are fitness junkies. That still gives you the experience of giving up an addiction, but in a much less dangerous way.

So what does all of this have to do with fear? Fear keeps us from these experiences that would make us better. Experience makes us more understanding and empathetic. These are key traits when it comes to relationships as human beings. They help us see what the real issue is so we know where to focus time and energy in a cause we believe in. Fear keeps us from experiencing the full spectrum of emotions. There is more to life than just fear. We can't fully experience joy until we take a risk to push beyond fear. There is a depth that comes from going that extra distance.

Fear keeps us from experience. Experience is the ultimate teacher. You don't know what you don't know until you dive in and live it for yourself. Although on occasion, fear IS the experience. Sometimes a little bit of fear can give us more understanding and empathy for others. Having fear of an experience will certainly lead to fear during it as well, but it is interesting how it can change. Let me clarify this with an example.

Being homeless was never anything that I thought would logically happen, but I figured it would be a terrifying experience and not one I was looking to have. Yet it did happen. The only reason I wasn't afraid of being homeless is because I never saw it as a possibility for me and my life. Had I seen it as a possibility, I would have been afraid. Then it happened and I experienced a whole new level of fear and understanding.

Before becoming homeless I didn't know how hungry I would be with no place to store or cook food. I didn't know how exhausted I would be because I was terrified of what was going on around me. I could be kicked out of where I was sleeping, I could be carried off, I could be attacked. These were especially scary as a woman. And without good, consistent sleep, I can now see why mental illness is so prevalent among the home-less population. These are important things that I didn't fully realize until I lived it for myself, and my fears were an important part of that knowledge that I gained.

While I had fear of the experience, and a significant amount during it, I do not fear it happening again. Not because I don't think it's a possibility. It is a very real possibility. I'll never discount that again, but rather I don't fear it because in that terrifying time, I saw the goodness of people. Oh, I saw plenty of the rottenness of some people, of that I have no doubt. However, I saw people who were willing to extend a hand in providing me a simple meal, which can go a long way when you are hungry.

In addition to food, I have learned how important relationships are. Having quality, healthy relationships would make a big difference in that scenario. Whether it be a friend willing to let me crash on their couch, let me borrow their shower, or even just hanging out with me at a park for conversation, or watching to make sure nothing happens while I grab a quick nap. I know that I have an arsenal should my life get to that point ever again.

Most importantly, I know I can survive it. I have done it once, I know I can handle it again. I know how to be prepared. When you know what to expect and how to handle it, it's harder to be afraid. Experience allows you to know and prepare much more than you would have the first time around.

Strength

Each experience and run in with the things that we fear make us stronger. I am a much stronger person in many ways for the time I spent homeless. Maybe not physically, but mentally and emotionally. What a confidence booster to know that I survived this once, and I can survive it again. It doesn't matter what the fear is, but living through it once gives you a sense of pride and accomplishment. Not only that, but next time around, you will have a better idea of what to expect, a better grasp of how to respond and a better idea of how to help others.

Each of these is an added measure of strength. We often refer to confident people as strong. Remember how the definition of courage is not the absence of fear? Having courage doesn't mean that fear will be completely gone. It just means you have a better game plan. Just because I wouldn't be afraid of being homeless again doesn't mean I wouldn't be afraid while homeless again. There are still very real physical dangers that come with being homeless. However, I am confident that I would have enough knowledge and resources to get me through them.

It is also a sense of pride to me that I was able to survive being homeless. This is an experience many don't have, either by never being homeless or never getting out of that situation. I am very fortunate to be one who has had both parts of that equation. It was hard and I can do hard things. That statement then translates into other areas of my life. "I can do hard things" becomes a lifestyle. I can do hard things at work. I can do hard things in relationships. I can do hard things in any area of my life.

Part of that strength comes from having a plan and knowing how to create one when things go wrong. The ability to solve problems is key to a successful life. It is needed in two different aspects: knowing how to prevent those issues from arising in the first place, and knowing how to create a plan when things do go wrong. Fear can actually help you with both. Fear is very good at foreseeing things that could go wrong and how to avoid problems. If you are afraid of snakes, stay away from certain regions and climates where snakes live. If you are afraid of heights, it's probably not a good idea to go skydiving. Afraid of getting fired at work? Work your tail off, find out what you need to do to stick around.

Our brains are naturally hardwired for defense when it comes to fear. We will stay out of scary situations no matter what it takes, so prevention is pretty much covered thanks to fear. The other side of the coin, however, is knowing what to do when things do go wrong. You can't plan for and prevent everything. Life has a very good way of making sure we still have to stare our fear directly in the face. It doesn't matter how good of a driver you are, there are other people on the road that make it a very real possibility that you could die in a car accident.

Things still happen and facing our fears helps to teach us how to respond at a moment's notice. The three natural responses to fear are fight, flight and freeze. Most of the time, I have a tendency to freeze. However, there are some situations where the best course of action may be to run away. Maybe the best action is to stand your ground. The more experiences we have, the more we can learn about our natural reaction to a situation and how to make sure that it is the best one. Just because I have a tendency to freeze, does not mean that it is the best option. At least not every time. There have been instances where that has come in handy. But that doesn't mean every time it is the best choice.

I have learned through years of abuse in relationships that I don't have to just freeze and take whatever the other person sends my way. In previous relationships, I would freeze when things started getting too physically intimate. I was uncomfortable, but didn't know what to do. I was paralyzed by the fear. That does not mean that the cycle has to continue. I am stronger now that I know how to respond to those situations. I have changed that tendency to freeze into an opportunity to stand my ground and stick to my standards. It may take time and a lot of hard work, but again, that ability to change my instinct and think in the face of fear, rather than freeze, has helped me across the board in many other areas of my life.

It is important to know how you respond and how to create the response you want when terrifying situations come your way. Life is hard. You have dealt with some scary things. Life follows a pattern of progression, though. Meaning the things we deal with are only going to get bigger and scarier. Which leaves us with few options. Either these situations win, and we fall deeper and deeper behind, constantly feeling buried under the weight we carry, or we learn to fight back. Throw our own punches once in a while, which will lighten our load a bit.

Either way, we need strength. Facing our fears is what will give us that power. We have the power to stare down our greatest fears, and do what needs to be done anyways. Conquering smaller fears voluntarily gives us strength when facing the ones we don't choose to face and will possibly never conquer. And that is okay. We need to understand that fear is a part of life. It is not always something that completely goes away. It is our relationship to fear that makes us stronger and determines the outcome. Our relationship to fear is a determining factor of our failure or success.

➤ IMPORTANCE OF RISK

Fear always comes when there is a chance of failure. Despite all of the experiences I've had in my life, what I regret is my constant aversion to risk. For many years I tried to play things safe. Any kind of scary situation that arose in my life, I tended to run or hide. I also was living only a half life. While that came with the absence of failure, sitting on the fence and going through the daily routine got kind of boring. It wasn't enough. There were things that I wanted in my life. No matter how much I looked at it and analyzed it and planned for it, I couldn't find any fail proof way to get what I wanted. The more time I wasted looking at fail-proof ways to get what I wanted was time that I could have been chasing after it, rather than looking from afar.

The great thing about risk is you always get closer to your goal. You learn what works and what doesn't. You don't have to succeed the first time. It's that first step that is the scariest, and that risk is always worth it. Not taking a risk is simply a guaranteed way to never get what you want and is the most common form of failure. When you face the terrifying choice of if you should take a risk or not, the real question is do you want a 100 percent chance of failing by NOT taking the risk, or do you risk success?

Another benefit of taking risks is the experience you gain along the way. Many people who are risk averse never fully experience anything. For example, there are many people who have a desire to write a book. The majority of people never take the risk to actually do it, and stop at various stages of the writing and publishing process. Some have ideas that they never sit and write. Some may have several drafts, but nothing completed. Those that manage to complete a manuscript, let it sit and collect dust rather than figure out the publishing process. Of those that manage to publish, even fewer find the success of having it sell well.

Each step is a learning process in itself. Each book I publish, I learn something new in almost every step. I continue to learn and improve in this endeavor. This is the third book I have published and it is by far my best. My next book is going to be even better though. I continue to take risks by spending my time writing, editing, publishing and selling books. Each time I learn something new in the process. Each time I get a little better. Each time is just as terrifying as the time before. For the past month, I've been recording how much time I have actually sat and worked on this book. It's far less time than I thought I was putting into it. I am still scared every time I sit to write.

It's hard to write something you are hoping lots of people will read. How terrifying is it to think that people will be reading some of my most personal experiences. I'm putting those things I've failed at out for the entire world to know about. Then comes editing. Where I realize that everything I've written is junk. My words go through a purifying process to make sure my words are clear and able to express the things that I've learned. Publishing? If you ever want to feel insecure about what you are doing, publish a book. You get to experience fears such as, "What if no one reads it?" and "What if people do read it and hate it?" or "Is what I'm writing even important?"

Yet this is a process that I repeatedly put myself through time and time again. When I hit "publish" on my very first book that I put on Amazon, *Awkwardly Strong,* I got such a rush. I did it. I did something many people dream of doing, but never do. It was exhilarating to know that I was officially a published author and to see what happens next. I've never been an adrenaline junkie. I'm not one to go bungee jumping or skydiving. I don't seek the thrill of extreme sports in any way. But hitting publish, I finally understood why they do it.

Facing something that you fear and doing it anyways is thrilling. It doesn't even matter what the outcome may be. Pass or fail, you overcame the fears leading up to it and you did it. You jumped. You published. No matter what it is that you fear, there is an inexplicable feeling that comes from facing it and doing it anyways. It's knowing you took a risk despite fear and the possibility of failure. Which honestly, already makes you a success. It doesn't matter how many copies of my first book sold. I've already hit a huge milestone that was worth celebrating. You have already hit a milestone worth celebrating.

➤ Importance of Change

Change is a scary thing. There are so many things that are unknown. Could it really be better than what you have now? What if it's worse? Things may not be perfect now, but it's comfortable. You know exactly what you are dealing with. You know what parts will be hard and which ones are just fine. So why do we even need that change? Isn't it a good thing to know what you are dealing with?

Maybe. While it's helpful to know what you are dealing with, it's also important to not get comfortable. It sounds weird and a little backwards, I get it. Comfort is a good thing and we naturally seek it. I'm not saying to never be comfortable again. However, comfort is a short sighted view. Sometimes we get too busy and frustrated and fill in the blanks here and there with any other type of emotion that we need a break from. Comfort is great for resting and recuperation. Then after a short breather, we are able to dive back into this chaos we call life.

Whether we like it or not, things will change. That's just a constant fact. It's just not possible for things to stay exactly as they are. Someone new starts at your work. A neighbor or friend moves away. New books are written and read. New movies are made and watched. News stories are always developing with some new tragedy in the world or another. These are just a few examples of things that can change.

Since things are constantly changing anyways, wouldn't you rather be in charge of what kind of changes are happening? At least some of them. We obviously can't control what happens in the world at large. Wouldn't you rather be spending the time and energy becoming better rather than simply keeping your head above water, barely keeping up with life and trying to keep things the same? Make the change, rather than letting the change make you.

We fear the unknown. We don't know what is coming and we don't know how to react or respond. We like to know these things in advance at all times. We want to know the ending before we really even start the adventure. We hate spoilers when it comes to books and movies, we want to experience the story. So why do we want spoilers for our own lives, rather than experiencing them fully and completely? The benefit of living your story is the added layer to your senses. And while movies are becoming more realistic all the time, they are not reality.

You don't get the same experience when you look at a picture of a mountain as you would if you actually climb one. You don't get the beads of sweat trickling down your face, showing the hard work you have put into the climb. You don't feel the warmth of the sun or the refreshing breeze that soothes the warm skin. You don't smell the fresh cedar trees or the salty ocean air. You don't get to taste the food made fresh in the remote village you have travelled with their unique blend of spices and different cooking styles. You don't get to have all of your questions answered by a local and hear their unique stories and the life they have lived.

The biggest problem is you only get what is fed to you. I love books and movies. Stories are great, but you don't get the choices that would enrich your experience. You don't get a choice in how you experience or handle the changes within the story. You passively sit and allow things to unfold in front of you. But to truly take hold of your fear and take control in your life, you need to be an active participant, rather than a spectator.

This is easier said than done, because again, we don't have any way of knowing how things will turn out. But at the same time, we do have more control and influence over how things end when we are actively pursuing an end goal. We may not know how or what we are doing, which can lead to a lot of failure along the way, but that really just leads me to my next point.

➤ IMPORTANCE OF FAILURE

This is one of my biggest fears. Who wants to fail? We end up looking ridiculous, we don't get what we wanted, we let other people down, we lose money… The list could go on and on of things we lose when we fail. Every choice we make is a bit of a gamble— we might win, we might lose. There is always a chance of success and a chance of failure. Most people have stopped even making the choice in order to avoid that failure.

I grew up outside of Las Vegas, Nevada, and have watched my fair share of gambling. Most people don't start out afraid of failure. It starts out innocent-ly enough, just putting down a few dollars. And then it's gone. They make the choice to keep playing. Again and again and again, they lose a few more dollars. Then the amount of money they have lost instills a sense of fear—they have to win. They have to get their money back, they have lost too much at this point. Especially those who don't know how to play the game.

I watched a lot of failure growing up. Always as a spectator, because I was one of those who didn't make the choice. I didn't want to risk failure. I didn't want to be one of those who lost thousands of dollars. I didn't want to be the reason we lost a game in sports. I didn't want to see myself as less than other people. I was afraid of what I saw. There were several problems with this. First off, I was watching bad examples of failure with the gambling. Secondly, I was comparing myself to others and pinning my worth on my success. I thought that I only had worth if I was succeeding at everything I did. I had to be perfect.

Great news, I am not perfect. Even better news, my worth as a human being does not depend on every single act resulting in success. Neither does yours. Life is a learning process and the best way to learn is to fail. The harder you fail, the more you learn. The people I was watching gamble away their life savings didn't learn. They charged ahead, never taking the time to consider the cost or figure out how to win the game. World-champion poker players don't just sit and play a lot. They study out strategies and techniques and learn from every game they lose. Because even world champions fail. The difference is that they learn and improve from it.

The same goes for anyone who has achieved any level of success. They failed an awful lot to get there. Then they looked at what went wrong and how they can improve. That's why athletes spend years practicing and perfecting strategies and techniques. That's why musicians do the same. I came across one of the best pieces of advice while working at a gymnastics academy. You don't practice until you get it right, you practice until you can't get it wrong.

Failure is a great teacher, as long as we are looking at what we are doing wrong so that we can go back and correct it. There is no better way to learn what works and what doesn't than to fail. In fact, I read recently in Darren Hardy's *Compound Effect* that success is one of the fastest ways to failure. When you do something once and it goes really well, you have no idea how to repeat that success again and again. He also discusses how wealth has a tendency to skip a generation (or more) because the hard work and failures that lead to the wealth in the first place don't get passed down.

The best thing you can do for yourself is to fail, fail often, and improve from each failure. This is easy to say in theory but harder to put into practice. It's one thing to study how to play the piano. One can know all the music theory, the 88 keys of the instrument, the various chords and what they sound like. However, it is a different story to feel the movement in your fingers as you play and to make sure your fingers hit the correct spot.

Several years ago, I had a couple friends from different places and times of my life all end up at Banff National Park in Canada. Their pictures were beautiful. The water was so clear, the grey mountains towering over the lush green forests and their happy faces piqued my interest about this place and I wanted to go. Seeing their pictures and reading about it did nothing to prepare me for the grandeur of this place. This isn't just a place you look at the beautiful photos and say, "Cool story, bro." This is a place that can't fully be appreciated until you hear the roar of the waterfall, feel the spray of cascading water and the rush of adrenaline as your foot slips for a moment before you continue the rest of the hike. Yes, I took a lot of photos, but they pale in comparison to the experience.

Failure does the same thing. It is something that is best felt and experienced to realize that it isn't the end of the world when it happens. That worst case scenario you imagine in your head? Nothing like the actual experience. Whether that image is the one I just attempted to create in Banff or failure of an actual project, you are wrong. Failure, and any experience really, requires full commitment. All the senses must be engaged to get the depth of what is really going on around you.

Artists who try to capture the feeling of something, no matter what medium they use—words, photography, paint, music—will all fail, no matter what they create, to fully capture that divine moment of inspiration. Yet we do it anyway. We write, compose, sing, paint and draw anything you can imagine. We get close. Good works of art are moving and profound in one way or another. Yet they still fall short of the true experience—the master teacher.

IDENTIFY AND NAME
YOUR FEAR

Self-Fulfilling Prophecies

IN ORDER TO MOVE FORWARD with life despite our
fears, we first have to know what they are. There are
so many different things that can scare us. Some of
them are so deeply rooted, they are more of a personal
belief rather than a fear. We may fear failure so much
that it has turned into a personal belief that we aren't
good enough and won't succeed at anything we do.
This is a false statement.

These fears then often become a self-fulfilling
prophecy. My friend Zach once mentioned to me that
he is often so afraid of freezing up when he is talking
to girls that when he starts talking to girls he likes, that
thought is all that consumes his mind. Since that is all
he can think about, he is unable to hold a conversation.
I was absolutely surprised to learn this fact, since Zach
is one of the best conversationalists I know. He goes
from one extreme to another, a great conversationalist

to having nothing to say. In essence, he freezes because he is afraid of freezing. If this was not such a fear, he would be able to talk to the girls he is interested in.

Knowing what you are afraid of and why will help you to stop forecasting your own failure, which can get in the way of what you want to do most. The deeper these are rooted, the harder they may be to identify or change, so keep that in mind as you read on. I have outlined a few of the most deep seated fears in the following sections. Be sure to take some time to look at what is holding you back from going after your dreams and which of these fears have turned into beliefs or self-fulfilling prophecies.

Fear of Self

This is a very subtle fear. How can you be afraid of yourself? It's not like you can hide from yourself. Yet it is very real and very common. We have a tendency to distract ourselves rather than spend time looking at who we have become. We are afraid of what we will see when we sit down and look at our life and the choices we have made. We tend to have very high standards for our life and fear how far off the mark we are.

How often do you spend time alone? And when you are alone, how much of that is distracted so you don't have to do much thinking? How much of that time are you busy with something like cooking, cleaning, reading, listening to music, watching TV or one of the other million things to do with your time besides just sitting and thinking? Do you journal at all? If we don't spend time alone with ourselves, we can't get to know what we really want and how to get it.

Spending time alone forces us to really look at who we are. Sometimes, we don't like what we see. So rather than figuring out a way to change it, we belittle and berate ourselves. We feel inadequate and that we are not enough. We tell ourselves just how awful we are, when really the opposite is true. In fact, sometimes we don't see that the real fear is how incredibly powerful we can be.

Marianne Williamson in her book *Return to Love* said, "Our deepest fear is not that we are inadequate. Our deepest fear is that we are powerful beyond measure. It is our light, not our darkness that most frightens us. We ask ourselves, 'Who am I to be brilliant, gorgeous, talented, fabulous?' Actually, who are you not to be?"

The hard part is that when we have to lead others, the responsibility returns to a fear of failure. Are we good enough? Are we going to screw up another person's life? Am I going to let things go to my head? We are so worried about being perfect that we miss the entire point of what we are doing. We are scared of how we come across to others. For some it might be that we are "too good" and a goody-two-shoes. For others it's that we aren't good enough, always reaching for the elusive state of perfection.

Being constantly afraid of our image and ego takes a lot of energy away from the things that are most important. Rather than focusing on how others see us, we should focus on the things that are most important to us. We hesitate to do things because we might come across as "wrong." No matter what we do, we are always going to be "too much." This applies to our appearance and how we look as well. We will always be too tall, too short, too different, too average, too experienced, too inexperienced, too pretty, too plain.

There are many "too much" phrases that we have heard and will hear throughout our lives. These phrases can be dangerous if we let them create fear in our lives. All they really mean is that we are too much for someone else to handle. But guess what? You are not here for them. You are here for you. How others view us does not matter. All we can do is be the best version of ourselves, and no one else can tell us what that means.

We need to spend time alone with ourselves to determine what our best looks like. I get that it is difficult to do, especially in the world that we live in. There are so many things to do and so little time to do it in. Even if we are alone, we are focused on things others have created. We may be reading a book, watching a TV show or movie, scrolling through social media or shopping online. Maybe we are even creating something. Maybe you are a writer, an artist, or an athlete. Just because you spend time alone doesn't mean you are spending time with yourself.

This is where things like meditation are important. You need to know what things are most important to you. The values that are a priority, the things you want to do, the person you want to become. These are things we need to know if we want to be truly strong mentally and emotionally. Knowing these things shapes the direction our lives take. They help us live a purposeful life with a focus and intensity that others do not have. It's fairly easy for people watchers to spot those who have a direction and purpose. They make decisions and take control of the life around them, rather than just going with the flow, wherever life takes them. They know who is in control and they work hard for it.

Thanks to history, we see what power can do to people. It can be addicting and have terrible consequences when that power is abused. This has caused society to swing in the completely opposite direction. We fear power, even if that power is in ourselves. However, the fear should be directed at the improper use of that power. To have control of your own life and taking that power you have is actually a good thing. Especially if we know how to utilize it to help others.

We are powerful creatures. We know it. That's why we have a fascination with superheroes and leading characters in our favorite books and movies. We admire the hard things they go through and the power they possess to move through it. They have power and they use it. We have that same power. It can be terrifying to see how much power we really have when we live with intention. It can also be upsetting to look at where we are and know how much more we could be doing with our lives.

Human beings are really good at avoiding things we don't want to face. We can bury it so deep that we don't even recognize what is really going on. This is where the fear of the self lies. No matter which direction you swing, the fear of self is very real. Do not be afraid of your own power. Become the superhero in your life. Be the superhero someone else needs by showing them how to live that power.

Fear of Awkward

This is one of my favorite topics. I love awkward. It took me a long time, but I finally figured out the secret to it! No one really likes awkward situations because they don't know what to do with them. The world we live in is full of unspoken societal rules. These rules are what we call culture. It's just what we do and we don't think about it. It has been the same since we were little and it is so basic and part of who we are that we don't even question why we respond to things the way we do.

So when, for example, someone hypothetically screams in the middle of a funeral, no one really knows what to do. Most funerals that I have been to are fairly quiet, reflective and sorrowful. So a joyous shout comes as a bit of a shock. People don't know how to respond or what to do. Who could be so excited at the passing of a family member? Someone with Tourette Syndrome, that's who. But if other people don't know that, the situation just gets awkward. If the shouts stop, enough time will pass that the service will just continue as normal. I might get a few glares from people close by who assume that I am rude and disrespectful. I would feel awkward long after the initial tic though.

However, if we take this same situation, and people know that I have Tourette Syndrome, I can hear the whispers passed along to inform the offending glares, "She has Tourettes." That is sufficient to stop any glares and I again feel comfortable in the situation, as do others around me.

That initial sense of awkwardness felt by both me and those around me was simply a lack of one of those unspoken rules I mentioned. No one knows what to do in this situation. The situation simply needs someone to take control of the situation so others know how to respond. Once one person steps up to take control of the situation and provide a set of rules to work within, the awkwardness goes away. Once someone knows the rules, they understand similar situations and pass the rules along (like the whispers I mentioned before). With this "rule" and understanding set in place people know how to respond which eliminates the awkwardness.

This doesn't just apply to Tourette Syndrome, that's just how I learned about it. It can apply to any awkward situation where we don't know the unspoken rules. For example, dating is full of incredibly awkward situations. No one has any idea what is going on there. Awkward moments can happen at work, at school… any situation. But now that you know the secret of how to handle awkwardness, you get to make the rules and create the outcome.

It may not always work exactly like you want it to, there are still people who will glare and say that Tourette Syndrome is made up or think I am possessed by a demon, but it takes away the initial awkward feeling and replaces it with anger. I know how to handle anger. I know the rules that I work within to maintain as peaceful of a scenario as possible, rather than punching the person in the face. Though both actions I suppose are understandable.

Facing an awkward situation can certainly be terrifying if you don't know how to handle it. So, now that you know what is going on, you can start to get ideas about how to handle things when no one else knows what is going on. Rather than consistently being afraid, work on changing your response. Make it into something funny that you and others can enjoy or find a way to change the topic. You decide what kind of response you want to have. I can't tell you what is best, but humor works best for me personally. It's easy to make others laugh when things get awkward and I love the memories it creates. So when I trip and fall, rather than turning red, I stand up tall and yell, "It's ok everyone, gravity still works!" This not only takes the attention off the fact that I can't walk in a straight line without falling over, but it makes others laugh and smile. People are more prone to remember the funny joke than the fact that I fell. More importantly, the awkwardness has disappeared because I took control of the situation. I don't wait to respond to what others are going to do or say. I make sure I have the first say. I don't wait for them to make a joke about my lack of coordination or rub in the fact that I fell.

For me, the scariest part about awkward moments is not knowing what rules are going to be created or used at the moment. Timidity and fear are actually more self-fulfilling prophecies like I mentioned earlier. Don't let others be the ones to make the rules. Take control and make the rules up yourself. It will certainly take time to play around with it and figure out what works best for you, but awkwardness has now become one of my favorite things and is no longer something I fear.

Fear of Hurt

This one is certainly hard. First off, there are two kinds of hurt. Physical pain, of course, and emotional pain. Both can be scary, especially if you don't have much experience with either. For some, physical pain isn't a big deal. However, I am a complete wuss and will treat both types of pain like the terror that they bring.

Hurt lets us know that something is wrong so that we can fix it and change things. It doesn't matter which pain we are referring to. Physical pain, such as putting your hand on a hot stove, tells us, "Umm, excuse you, move your hand NOW!" If we don't follow that instruction, we deal with terrible consequences. If we never moved our hand from the hot stove, that heat would eventually burn away the hand completely.

It's not just about the pain, it's also about the consequences. Emotional pain can act the same way. In a dating relationship, if we are ignored, it hurts. If it happens, and the more frequently that it does happen, it is a fairly simple sign that the relationship is not a healthy one and you need to get out of it. Pain is simply a warning that there are terrible consequences ahead and you need to move.

So of course it would be something scary. No one wants to deal with that in small or large doses. However, pain is a common part of life and something that we have to learn to deal with. Remember how I'm a wuss and hate pain? I don't like this idea any more than you do. That doesn't change the fact that it is simply reality. We cannot keep ourselves in some kind of plastic bubble that protects us from any and all pain.

While that bubble can protect us from most physical pain, it does nothing for emotional hurt. When we push away relationships with people because we are afraid of getting hurt, we create another type of pain—loneliness. When looked at logically, we guarantee pain if we constantly shy away from relationships. We ensure that we will be haunted by the pain of loneliness the rest of our lives. And remember, pain is a sign that we are doing something wrong and something needs to change.

If we are willing to take a risk on people and relationships, there is a large chance that we will get hurt. But what if this one is different? What if this is the friend you need to get through a rough patch? What if this is the relationship that makes you want to start a family? And because it involves two humans, and humans are imperfect, there will be pain. Even the best relationships will have pain. But again, it's simply a sign that something is wrong and needs to be dealt with properly. That does not mean abandoning the relationship every time. That can also mean there is a disagreement that requires some discussion before a conclusion can be made.

While relationships are obviously the easiest example to give, this idea applies to so many areas of life. Apply it to whatever area of your life needs it most. Rejection is painful, whether that is from another person, getting turned down for a promotion at work, not getting into the school you wanted to attend, or something else. Take any kind of pain you are dealing with and look at what causes it. Pain isn't something to fear, that pain is your ally to help you live your best life. If there is pain, it just needs some attention and a few tweaks here and there. The bigger the pain, the more of an overhaul you are going to have to make. But that also means the more you are really going to love what is on the other side of that pain.

Fear of Good Things

This one is really ironic, but very real. Most people wouldn't really be afraid of something good happening, where is the sense in that? Of course we want good things to come our way. Yet actions and decisions we make every day reaffirm that this is a very real thing. We may think we want good things but our actions say differently.

When opportunities arise, we hang back in fear. Say a position at work opens up with better pay and better hours. It would be perfect for you. Do you apply? Are you chasing after the things you want in life? We may not feel worthy of it, someone else is applying and they are sure to get it, you aren't what they are looking for... does this sound familiar?

While we want the opportunities and the perks, we don't want the risk. And all good things require taking risks. We are afraid of the requirements that come with good things in life. As stated by Rumplestiltskin in the television series *Once Upon A Time*, "All magic comes with a price." And all good things are magical. While Rumplestiltskin meant it as a warning for the negative side effects of magic, the statement works both ways.

All good things do come with a price. Sometimes in the form of hard work, sometimes in exchange for money, but always involving effort and risk on our end. We are afraid of the cost. We are afraid of the commitment. What if we put in all of this time, money, work, etc. into one thing just to find out that we missed another opportunity somewhere else? We have this tendency to fear missing opportunities and to search for perfection in every result. While there have never been so many opportunities available, the search for perfection has always plagued humankind.

According to Kenneth Burke's *Definition of Man*, "Man is the symbol-using (symbol-making, symbol-misusing) animal, inventor of the negative (or moralized by the negative), separated from his natural condition by instruments of his own making, goaded by the spirit of hierarchy (or moved by the sense of order), and *rotten with perfection*" (emphasis added). While perfection can be a good thing, sometimes the pursuit of, as well as the misunderstanding of perfection, can have disastrous results.

In our time, we are starting to see a shift in the view of perfection, meaning that there are so many ways that this could go wrong and allow our fear to take over. Seeking perfection, and especially misunderstood perfection, makes us afraid to take a wrong step. We can't do it at all unless it's going to be perfect. We constantly feel eyes looking over our shoulder at everything we do. How will this look in a social media post? What would God think? The government is out to get me, I have to watch my step. No matter what eyes you think are watching you, you feel the need to watch your back and to have perfection in every step.

In recent times, this fear of perfection has taken a new turn. We can be so afraid of the paralyzation caused by fear that we go the opposite direction. We fear the control and takeovers caused by those seeking perfection, so we stay out of them completely. I'm guilty of this one myself. Looking at an extreme example, Nazi Germany was the result of those seeking perfection. They showed clearly and plainly that the search for perfection can be tumultuous to say the least. They instilled so much fear. Some were simply afraid for their lives and fighting to live another day. These are the stories we focus on the most. However, there were also those afraid to step up and do something about it, those that were afraid of what the Nazi party stood for and its takeover, and those that were seeking perfection in line with the protocol but were afraid of making a misstep. We are human, we make all sorts of mistakes.

In order for things to be perfect, there is no room for anything else except that vision of perfection. There is no room for mistakes. There is no room for differences. There is no room for creativity. Yet often in the mistakes, we can find something better than our vision of perfection.

In Japan, there is a beautiful art form called kintsukuroi. As ceramic dishes crack due to age or being dropped, rather than throwing away the pieces that have been broken, they are repaired. The mending process fills in the gaps from the cracks with gold, silver or platinum. The results are often beautiful and increase the value of the overall product. The belief behind this practice is that rather than disguising and hiding the flaws, the history of the object should be acknowledged.

Each decision we make is part of our own personal histories. We are human and we make mistakes. But rather than clutching at the wounds caused by our mistakes and never trusting ourselves with decisions, we can utilize those failures and line them with golden successes. Just because we make mistakes doesn't mean we can't obtain a different form of perfection than we originally thought. Seeking perfection is only dangerous when we close doors to ourselves and do not allow the good things to show us another version of perfect.

Even when we fall short of perfection, we can still obtain good things in our lives. No matter what the dream or goal is, it's going to be good. Not just good, but wonderful and it brings a form of perfection that makes it incredibly worth the risk. So much so that in looking back, we only wonder why we waited so long in the first place.

A second way we show we fear good things is by not feeling worthy. Coming from someone who dealt with depression as a teenager, I can very much verify the reality of this concept. Feelings of our own self worth can also hold us back from the desired life we want. When we make those missteps and fall short of perfection, we think we deserve it.

Even if we have done nothing wrong, we still don't feel like we deserve any form of goodness. It's as if we think there is a finite amount of good things in this world and that there are others who deserve much more than we do. We shove away opportunities thinking someone else deserves it more. However, I want to let you in on a secret. There is no end of good things in this world. Success does not have a finite supply. Just because you succeed does not mean others will have to fail. There is an ebb and flow in life, which will bring periods of success and periods of difficulty. You are allowed to take yours once in a while. Allowing for success and good things in your life does not make you a bad person. It doesn't make you selfish.

My cousin Anslin and I are best friends and we were especially close in high school when we lived in the same town and saw each other every day. Anslin was the girl in high school everyone wanted to be like. In a small town, everyone noticed, too, because she did it all. She played soccer, several instruments, sang like an angel, was the lead in the school play, got good grades, was beautiful, yet also managed to be kind and inclusive of other people. Not only that, but she was often asked to serve in leadership positions in church, which she was always willing to do. This was during a time when I dealt with depression, and I would often compare myself to her and my thoughts often spiraled out of control. Why wasn't I that good? At *anything?*

Here is where I had some flawed thinking. I was young after all. Just because she was good at the piano, doesn't mean I wasn't good at the violin. We both got good grades, we both sing well. We are family and look fairly similar. Where we differed was her fearless pursuit of everything. I didn't dare try out for sports because I didn't think I was good enough (probably because I never practiced) and I never would have been able to stand in front of a crowd for the school play.

Lucky for me, this did start to change once I got to college. Funny how we learn as we grow older. Turns out, I am known for my love of dancing and can pick it up quickly (especially when I put in a lot of practice) and I can be on stage during plays (though I prefer musicals). I can also make informed decisions. I can be kind, considerate and inclusive to others because I'm not so worried about my own fears and how I will look to others. I can, and have, held leadership positions in church. I am just as needed in the world as Anslin is.

The point of explaining Anslin and my abilities is not to show off in any way. I want to emphasize my way of thinking and set the stage a bit. Because while we are very similar in a lot of ways, I always thought that she was better and deserved good things more than I did. When opportunities came my way, I had a tendency to shove Anslin into the spotlight.

Like the time at the Clark County Fair and Rodeo, we were watching a show choir performance from Southern Utah University. We were probably freshman in high school and were in awe at the talent (not to mention cute boys) up on the stage. At one point in the show, I remember making eye contact with one of said cute boys. So during the next song, when he was singing a solo and started walking towards me to pull me on stage, I quickly pointed to Anslin and she was pulled on stage, surrounded by talented, good looking guys while they serenaded her.

While this has had no long-lasting repercussions on either one of our lives, I have looked back and wondered why I was so afraid of something that my 15-year-old self would have loved and why I gave it away. It's not like I had to do anything, there was no pressure for me to perform. Why was I so afraid of a good thing? It's not like my cousin would have been upset with me. We would have giggled and talked excitedly about it no matter who got the experience. This fearful mindset slowly grew and took over my high school years, and much of it passed the same way.

When it came to crushes, the guys were more likely to like her, so I never bothered. When it came to auditioning for solos in choir, I never tried out. Any chances I had for good things, I gave away. There was more than one solo, and we both could have had one. As for boys, just because she liked them didn't mean I couldn't. Besides, what if a boy actually did prefer me and thought I didn't like him. I didn't flirt with guys she liked, even if I liked them, too. I can't change how someone feels about either one of us, so why did I automatically step down and think I had no shot?

I don't resent her in any way, I still love my cousin and she still loves me. Life has taken us down very different paths, and we both have successes in our own ways. We are still very similar in a lot of ways, but there are a lot of ways we are different. The world is big enough for both of us to share and explore. We can both be successful, and this isn't limited to just the two of us. There is enough success to go around.

Fear of Failure

This one is incredibly common and we all know it. No one WANTS to fail, right? Ironically, the more I study about becoming successful and reaching the goals I set, the more this is encouraged. In fact, the most successful people DO want to fail. Many self-help gurus point out and direct us to follow the example of famous success stories that faced rejection after rejection and failure after failure like Thomas Edison, J.K. Rowling, Steve Jobs, Albert Einstein, and even Walt Disney.

It was their failures that made them a success in one way or another. They exemplified all the traits that are required to become the legends that they have become. Perseverance. Dedication. Willingness to learn. Improvement. Without these traits, they wouldn't have created such high quality products or made discoveries that keep us coming back for more. Sure you hear of the few who got their lucky break... and became one-hit wonders. But those few are unable to consistently produce what got them there in the first place, or improve and build upon what they had.

If you really want to make a difference in your life, you will have to face the possibility of—and eventual—failure. The good news is that you will also see successes that will keep you moving forward. We will not catch every ball that comes our way, hit every note we play or charm every person we meet. But you will get increasingly better. You will see improvement. You will be more consistent with correct notes. You will have more friends. You will catch the ball more often. No matter what it is that scares you, getting it right makes it worth the failures that occur. Even if they are more frequent than the successes. The numbers don't matter, but the trying—and eventual success—does.

If you are afraid of failure, a great way to counter this is to study success. Find out what it is, how people get it and what it will take to get it for yourself. There have been many studies done on successful people and many books written about the subject. Since success is not the purpose of this book, I'll let you find those on your own, but by way of recommendation, you can start with a few of my favorites: *Willpower Doesn't Work* by Benjamin Hardy, *4 Commitments of a Winning Team* by Mark Eaton and *Think and Grow Rich* by Napoleon Hill. That is a good start, and from there, you can find many, many more.

FOMO

The fear of missing out (commonly called FOMO) is a relatively new phenomenon. FOMO, as a term or phrase, did not even exist at the beginning of the millenium. This has developed into a thing during the past ten years or so thanks to living in a hyper-connected world. We are suddenly more aware of everything going on, not just around us, but all over the world. I know I have felt this fear of missing out, and trying to keep up with it is quite frankly exhausting.

This is especially painful and debilitating when you have two (or more) things going on at the same time. We suddenly have this inability to miss out on anything that's going on. We want to do all the things with all the people. Take for example my Memorial Day weekend. An extra day off work was needed, and I had several things I wanted to do.

To start with, I had a group of friends going to the Grand Canyon for a camping trip. I've never been to the Grand Canyon and have a strong desire to go. What an opportunity! However, Memorial Day weekend this year fell on the birthday of a younger brother who passed away at birth. My family feels a strong connection with him and we wanted to get together to remember and celebrate him and to appreciate each other while we are still here. We were going to meet up in a little town in southern Utah. Both incredibly good options. But then you add in the factor that I have a tendency to work too hard and play too hard and part of me just wanted to stay home and rest.

How do you choose between three good options? I wanted to do them all, but that was obviously impossible due to geographic location alone. I stressed over this for weeks leading up to the weekend in question. At which point, I was so exhausted from stressing out over it, that I just stayed home and relaxed. Honestly, looking back, that was the thing that I needed most, even if I was missing out on something new and exciting (Grand Canyon) or profoundly meaningful (family time).

The ironic thing about all of this is that had I given in to the FOMO and done either activity, I would have exhausted myself even more. At which point, I couldn't have done many other things that were going on in June. There is physically no possible way to do all the things you want to do. It's frustrating, no doubt about that. However, it is much more rewarding to be able to do a few things well, than attempt to do everything halfway decent. This applies to everything, not just events to attend or projects to complete.

FOMO robs us of the quality of the experience. You may show up to an event, but are so exhausted that you aren't fully present in that moment. You miss out on the excitement, the happiness, the gratitude, the energy or any other emotion that you could be fully feeling if you were present. Same with projects you may be working on. There may be several, but again, when you spread yourself so thin you are more likely to miss details, bounce from project to project and never fully focus on one because of the others also floating around in your head. This leads to nothing ever getting completed.

It also creates stress and additional anxiety in our lives; further exhausting us and cutting into our ability to do things well. It turns into a vicious and dangerous cycle. While it may not appear to be a debilitating fear, it very much can be, especially the more we lean into this idea. Thinking we have to do everything is a form of perfectionism. We have this idea of who we are supposed to be and what we are supposed to do, which feeds this concept of FOMO. The two play off of each other.

Here is one of the most liberating secrets I have learned—the words "*supposed to*" are a man-made idea that isn't necessary. Even the Oxford dictionary defines it as "generally assumed or believed to be the case, but not necessarily so." Who said you have to be a certain way? Do a certain thing? Live a certain life? Who said it and why do they have control of YOUR life? You are the one who makes the choices about who you want to be and what you want to do. Just be sure you know the difference between want, need and supposed to do. The only things you really need to focus on are the things you need and the things you want, not what is expected of you.

There also needs to be a balance of want and need. This is where FOMO becomes a problem. If I lean too heavily into what I *want* to do, I forget the things I *need* to do. There is a bigger picture to look at before I jump into the things I want. I still need to go grocery shopping. I still need to clean my apartment. I still need to sleep. Don't miss out on these necessary things just because you would rather be doing something else.

Sometimes we have to say "no" and we have to miss out on things. We might miss out on a travel experience or a party. We can miss out on fun things when something important comes along. The reverse can also hold true. If you have a once in a lifetime opportunity to go on your dream vacation, you can miss a few days of work. The company won't shut down without you.

I remember the first time I ever skipped a class. I was in college, and was under so much stress. When I looked at all the things I had to do, I could get them done if I just had that one more hour rather than going to class. As much as I hated to do it, I skipped the class, nervous I had missed important information and I over exaggerated the consequences in my mind. I still passed the class, and took a huge load of stress off by getting everything complete. This may not be the most relatable example, but very real for a perfectionist with perfect attendance.

Remember how FOMO is a new phenomenon? For thousands of years, people have been missing out on so much because of time period limitations. Yet they survived. Several of them were even happy and led meaningful lives. I might even argue that they lived more meaningful lives than we do today because they weren't guided by FOMO.

Battling the FOMO requires taking a timeout from life to recenter yourself. There are many ways to do this, and you can choose what works best for you. Maybe it's yoga, meditation, journaling or taking a bubble bath with nothing on your mind. Essentially, it's time for you to take a break and just relax and recharge. Spend some quality time with yourself. Figure out what is most important and what is OK to miss out on. Don't just do this once, make it a weekly activity for yourself.

I see the irony in FOMO. Usually fear is what stops you from doing things. However, FOMO makes you want to do everything. It is still a very real fear and can still cripple us. Life is not just about doing all the things available to us, it's about doing them well. It means fighting fears not so you can do *everything,* but because doing so I add to the quality of your life, not take away from it.

TIPS TO HELP BEFORE

WE KNOW big and terrifying things will happen in life. That's not surprising. Although, what we should be preparing for is not the scary event itself, but rather how we are going to respond to it and what we will do when it happens. Being prepared can decrease our levels of fear significantly.

We can take that a step farther, too. If we take time to understand what we need in scary situations we know are going to happen, we can understand what we need to do when the unexpected happens. It's going to be different for everyone. Figure out what works best for you. Once you know what works for you, you can utilize that in situations where you are caught off guard. Fear does not have to immobilize you, and you can still have some control in how the situation plays out.

Preparation can certainly help when you have advance notice, but life doesn't always play fair like that. There will be times when you are surprised and thrown off guard. So be prepared for what you can, but be able and willing to just go with the flow. For example, have a savings account in case you are let go at work or the company goes under. No matter what situation life throws at you, you can at least be prepared financially to get the help you need.

When preparation is just not an option, we can still set ourselves up for success by understanding where we stand on certain issues. Rather than fearing death, whether for ourselves or for a loved one, we can figure out where we stand on the topic of life after death. I'm getting philosophical here, but that is something that has, again, helped me immeasurably. The first deaths in my life occurred when I was too young to really understand what happened. As a child, you don't really grasp why you can't take piano lessons because your teacher is gone, or why everyone is sad for someone they don't even know. I just didn't get it.

I was older when someone I knew and loved passed away. My grandpa died when I was a senior in high school, just a few months before I graduated. We all knew it was coming. My grandpa had been in bad shape for a few years. He had gotten to a point where he would get up in the morning and walk to the couch. Then, exhausted by the effort, he would sleep there the entire day. At the end of the day, he would wake up, walk to his bed and again sleep all night from the strain. It was hard on my grandma to take care of him in that state. It was hard for all of us to see this strong military man with a feisty sense of humor and strong will reduced to such a state.

By the time he passed away, it was almost a relief. My grandpa may have been here physically, but the man we loved was already long gone. Having grown up in a religious home, I believe in life after death. Watching the long drawn out process for my grandfather was in a way a huge blessing, at least for me. I was able to watch how death can, in a way, be a good thing. When someone has led a full life, death is a release from pain, physically, mentally and emotionally. Observing this aspect of death during this time helped me to cope and remove my fear of it.

Finding your own philosophies on things that terrify you will help you to prepare for unexpected situations. When we have a broader understanding about how the world works it can help us see the bigger picture. This bigger picture allows you to step back and see how everything is connected. Having this perspective is especially important when deciding if the fear is something protecting you or something you should take the time and effort to push past.

Philosophy and preparation take time and may sound silly, but I have yet to find anything better for helping one face their fears. They provide that extra measure of confidence, which most of the time is all we really need. At least for just a moment, you can be sure that everything will be fine, and it's during that moment, that your life can change.

Five Seconds of Crazy

Sometimes, all it takes is five seconds of crazy. I've already mentioned my fear of heights. Yet, while I was living in Hawaii, I had several friends who loved to go cliff jumping at the various waterfalls we would hike to and swim in. While I didn't often participate, there were occasions where they would talk me into climbing up and looking over the fresh, blue water below. The views were stunning. Then my friends would jump into the water below, while I stood frozen at the top.

Part of me wanted to jump as well, that has to be understood. This was not a case of peer pressure in any way. I was just terrified and immobile. I had friends who said they would stay up there with me until I jumped, or were even supportive enough to say they would help me climb down. But I did want to jump and refused to turn around and climb down.

My friends tried all sorts of encouragement. They would jump with me, they would take me out for ice cream after, they would talk about how amazing it felt and about getting out of the mosquitos hovering around…none of it really worked. I still stood there, frozen. Then, without warning, I jumped. I made the choice to just jump, but rather than take the time to inform my friends and "prepare," I just did it before I lost my nerve.

I couldn't think about it, I just had to do it. It took all of five seconds to make my muscles move. We often know what we have to do in the face of fear, but…fear. Rather than letting it take control and paralyze us from doing things we want or need to do, we should take Nike's advice and just do it. Stop thinking about all the ways it might go wrong. Stop thinking about how to do things right. Just move forward, then spend the time after to enjoy the experience or learn ways to do it better. Both options are much more pleasant than standing still in fear.

Deep Breaths

Stop what you are doing and take a breath. Allow it to give you a step back and see the situation around you clearly. Taking a deep breath has been proven to have many physical benefits that also help our state of mind. It reduces stress levels, heart rate and blood pressure just to name a few.

Think of what that could do for you in the face of fear. When everything is happening lightning fast, you can almost feel like you are slowing down time to get a good look at what is going on around you. Things will still happen quickly, but your ability to process and act will increase.

Taking a deep breath will bring a moment of peace and clarity. While it will only last a moment, it is enough to recenter your view of what is before you. No matter if you are facing danger fear or challenge fear, you will need a level head. You will come out of the situation far better than if you hadn't.

Let's look at an extreme situation and a common one. If you were in a burning building, suddenly surrounded by flames and heat, you would want to take a deep breath to calm down and figure out the best way out and maybe even be able to see if there is anything you should grab before you go. Without that deep breath to collect your thoughts, all we can see is the danger of the situation and how to get as far from it as possible. Even if that drives us further into the building rather than out of it. A deep breath will help you to act rather than simply react to the situation.

A more common case might be if you were suddenly surrounded by a lot of people, with all the movement, conversations and eyes on you as you stand in the midst. Situations like this can cause panic attacks, but a deep breath can help prevent or end one. This exercise might have to be repeated several times as you move through the crowd, but it will keep you from entering a full state of panic as you continuously breathe deep to lower that blood pressure and make yourself keep moving towards your destination.

Journal

Journaling is a great way to prepare to face your fears. It helps us to see them clearly and discover what fears exist below the surface. Understanding what we are afraid of can then help us see the best way to face them. It was through journaling that I discovered my fear of men. I had been writing, wondering why I act the way I do around them when I realized what was going on. It was then several years later, again while journaling, that I overcame that fear.

Journals are great places for reflecting and asking yourself questions. We often do not take the time to simply ask what is going on, and if we do, we don't really try to find an answer. If we have an answer, that means we have to act on it and make changes. Did you catch that formula? Ask a question → Find an answer → Act on that answer. I get it, that's a hard thing to put into practice. So we often just determine that we continue to live the way we do, and that is better than trying to face those fears.

However, if that were *really* the case, would you have even picked up this book? So often we put ourselves between a rock and a hard place. We don't want to live in fear, but we are afraid of moving forward. After a while, a decision will have to be made. You will either come to "accept your fate" as it is and continue to live in fear, or you will make a decision to push past the fear.

For the record, I don't believe that living in fear is a fate that you must accept. Fate means that something is out of your control and overcoming fear is not out of your control. You can do this, and telling yourself otherwise would be a lie to make you feel more comfortable. The lie helps us to justify our fear.

Another benefit of spending time writing in a

journal is that it helps us to discover the lies that we have told ourselves. Stopping and taking the time to really look at why we do the things we do and why we are afraid is so incredibly liberating. I could physically feel a weight being lifted off my shoulders as I journaled about my fear of men and that act helped me to overcome my fear.

It started off with me simply asking why. Why was I so afraid and what was I afraid of? Well, I was afraid of being taken advantage of. I was afraid of being used and manipulated. Why was I so afraid of that? Why did I automatically equate that with men? Simply put, because it had happened before and not just once. However, that was not *every* interaction with men. I then realized that those were the predominant experiences because I was shutting out all of the good men due to being afraid. It didn't have to be that way because there are good men in the world.

I then also realized that it really couldn't get much worse, I've already experienced my biggest fear, and I survived. Not only did I survive, but I had healed from it. I had become a better and stronger person. With the experiences I lived through, I have seen first hand what to watch for and what to avoid. I knew how I would have reacted differently in those circumstances and would be able to change the outcome if another instance came around. All of these realizations came because I was willing to spend the time writing in my journal and finding answers to my questions.

Support

Humans are social creatures. As the old adage says, "No man is an island." We need other people in order to be the best version of ourselves. This is especially important during times of fear, stress and anxiety. A lot of the fear comes from change. It can be incredibly scary to face the unknown, especially when we are comfortable where we are. Even when things seem awful, it is more appealing to avoid change than confront it because at least we know how to deal with it.

Having a good support system is key because change is inevitable. Things always change and having a support system makes all the difference. Sometimes we just get so stuck in our own heads and our own way of thinking. Your support system, be it family or friends, will be able to see things you can't because they aren't the ones going through the change. Without the lens of fear, they can see things a little differently and provide insight that we might miss as we navigate through change and terrifying situations.

I can't tell you the number of times I have been on the precipice of change and had friends and family talk me down to help me clear my head, or jump in and do what needed to be done. When I was a senior in high school, I couldn't even bear to think about life outside of my little hometown. I had grown up in the same place and had known the same people since kindergarten. I didn't know how to meet new people, I could barely talk to the ones I had known for years. I didn't know how to live on my own. There were a lot of things I didn't know and it all absolutely petrified me to have to face all of these things.

I was still undecided about what I really wanted to do with my life, so I mentioned to my mom that I might just stay home and work for a year to save my money. College is expensive, right? I could get a little more clarity if I took a year off, I would save on rent and tuition and have a little bit more of a jump start with that kind of preparation. I had a great job that I loved and a million other great reasons why I should put off leaving for a year.

However, my incredibly wise mother saw through all of the logic I had carefully (and fearfully) laid out. She had done the same thing out of high school. She had been valedictorian of her class and attended one of the first schools to have access to computers. She had a lot of opportunities, but she, too, was scared. She was also going to take a year off before going to college to think about what she wanted to do and all of the other reasons I had listed.

Turns out she never went to college at all. She has regretted it ever since. She was not about to let me make the same mistake. She was going to make me go to college and I could figure it out along the way. She reminded me of how much I loved school and how this really was something that I wanted. She wasn't about to let my fear get in the way. She wanted me to leave home, because she knew I loved to travel, but stay close in case of emergencies.

Turns out, there is a tiny college about a four hour drive from my hometown. Close enough for emergencies, far enough that I couldn't come home every weekend. Since it was a small junior college, tuition was cheaper than a larger university. Not only that, but my mom's best friend lived just ten minutes away so I had someone to watch over me and make sure I was getting enough to eat, etc.

Had my mom not suggested this place, which eradicated most of my fears, I might not have gone. Her insight and knowledge that I didn't have about this tiny school provided me with an opportunity for some of the best experiences of my life. I built upon those experiences and gained more and more confidence in trying new things. Now that I had some experience under my belt, I had less things to fear. I knew I could live alone, I knew how to do the college thing and I was able to easily transfer when the time came to go beyond little Snow College.

ANXIETY DURING

Sometimes life just likes to throw us curve balls and we have no time to prepare. We don't always have the chance to process fears with journaling or make sure we have a support system in place when and where we need it. That doesn't mean we curl up in a ball and cry (no matter how much we may want to). There are still ways to move forward, no matter what fear you may be facing.

Utilize the Fear as Adrenaline

This is the main point I want to emphasize. Fear, historically speaking, happened when there was a literal threat to life and survival. As I mentioned earlier, our bodies have a physical reaction in the presence of danger and fear. We get a rush of adrenaline and your body knows what to do when challenged. So why haven't our brains figured out how to utilize it?

That extra energy should be used for something more than just stress and heart palpitations. That fear becomes energy that should be used to help you survive and overcome whatever it is that scares you. Scared to present to the CEO of the company? Use that energy to prepare for your presentation. Scared to talk to a girl? Use that energy to walk towards her, not away from her.

When you take time to breathe and recognize the flow of adrenaline surging through your body, don't think of it as nerves. That is courage surging through your veins. If you let it, it can actually heighten your awareness of what is going on and what is needed. Sometimes, the body can even use that adrenaline rush to function as an auto-pilot and help you get through stressful situations.

There have been several times in my life when I was so terrified, my body went into auto-pilot. I was literally scared senseless and had no comprehension of what was going on around me or how I survived. The choices I made may not have been the best, but given the circumstances, the outcome could have been much worse.

Like the time I was the third, and last, car in a caravan driving up a mountain on an unfamiliar road. As we climbed in altitude, we came upon a semi truck that had slowed down significantly trying to get up the mountain. There was a passing lane for those needing to get around semi trucks that struggle trying to get up the hill so the flow of traffic can continue. So the first car in the caravan moved to the left and got in front of the truck, as did the second car, so I did the same. However, the cars in front of me were not going fast enough for me to get past the truck before the lane started to end. I couldn't speed up because of the cars in front of me. The semi truck started getting closer and closer and I didn't dare brake to get behind the truck and lose the caravan. None of us had cell phones and I had no idea where I was or where we were going to end up.

While I was busy panicking, my body just kept driving. I was in a really bad situation. I'm not sure exactly what happened, but I finally managed to get in front of the truck without running off the road and stayed with the group. This situation is not as likely to have had the same ending if I had not received a rush of adrenaline.

This was when I realized that what I have always called nervous energy is actually something that I can utilize and use to my advantage. The other simple steps mentioned above help me to move past my initial fear, but it is the adrenaline that pushes me through and allows me to accomplish things I never would have been able to do without it. Others have reported feats of superhuman strength in times of need, most likely because of fear and the adrenaline that comes with it. There are several examples of this, but one story is of Nick Harris, who back in 2009 lifted a car off of a little girl named Ashlyn. Nick doesn't have a history of lifting cars, or even performing great feats of strength. He simply saw what Ashlyn trapped and went to help in any way he can. Individuals like Nick were able to simply utilize the adrenaline to work for them rather than against them.

Distractions

We are often told that we should not distract ourselves from solving a problem and that distraction is a bad thing. However, I would disagree to an extent. I agree that while we should not distract ourselves from facing fears and problems, it can also be an effective tool when used properly.

For example, working at a gymnastics academy with a lot of children, I get to see human nature exhibited on a much more basic level. One day a kid was pushed and he fell and scraped his elbow. Of course, it hurt so the kid started screaming. The kid who did the pushing apologized, then the kid who was pushed came to the office so the coach could look at the extent of the damage. It was a small cut. So, we gave him a band aid and attempted to comfort him in order to get him back on the floor. He had no serious threat of harm or injury that needed attention and nothing that would cause lasting pain. However, the kid was inconsolable. He continued to scream as if the world was about to end. Eventually the coach had to get back on the floor for her class (and her sanity) and the kid was left in the office with me until he could calm down. I put him in the back office (where his screams wouldn't hurt my head—I mean, be heard as well) to sit on the couch. I would pop in every few minutes to see him still screaming at the top of his lungs and clutching his arm.

After a while, the office got busy and I didn't check

on him as often, but I could hear him moving around, occasionally he would peek outside the back office to see me and make sure I was still listening to his screams. I eventually told him that if he feels good enough to get up and move, he can go back to class. "BUT IT HURTS!!!" He was so focused on his pain and the consolation he wanted that it was all he could see. He clung to it and refused to let go. However, he was also getting bored of sitting in the office with no one paying attention to his screams.

I informed him that I thought it was time for him to go back to class and maybe if he moved around and stopped thinking about it, the scrape wouldn't hurt as much. Boy, did I get a death glare from him. He was not happy, and he continued to scream all the way to the floor. Though, I'm happy to report that the screaming stopped after about two minutes back on the gym floor.

If all we do is sit and focus on how awful and terrifying it is to face our fear, that's all we will see. We can kick and scream and cry all we want, but it still has to be done and all we are doing is extending that pain and fear. If we find something to focus on outside of this tunnel vision of the task at hand, we are better able to cope and move forward.

Let me share another example. Dealing with large crowds of people gives me some serious anxiety unless I know every person in the room, or at least a majority of them. Usually I do know most of the people and I'm quite comfortable in my social settings. My brain has this tendency to want to know everything at all times. It will try to see all the faces, hear all the conversations and understand the dynamics of every person in the room. If I know most of the people, I know the dynamics and personality traits already, so I can tune them out.

One weekend a few friends of mine decided to go swing dancing. I had been to this place before and had a great time. However, I failed to realize that I had gone on a weeknight, so when the weekend hit to go dancing, there were suddenly A LOT more people. I had an instant panic attack and sensory overload. The loud music, the flashing lights, the crowded room—mostly the crowded room—started to overwhelm me.

The instant I was pulled onto the dance floor to start dancing, I was given one thing to focus on—not tripping over my own feet. Don't get me wrong, I love dancing and am not too shabby at it, but it still takes concentration to move with the music and another human being. Focusing on dancing made most things fade away and evened out my senses.

Once the dance was over and the outside stimuli were reintroduced, my brain had already begun to process the stimuli and was no longer in overload. Rather than being overwhelmed, I was able to take in my surroundings like a "normal" person. My fears and anxiety significantly dropped.

In this case, just like with the little boy at the gym, we needed a distraction in order to help face our problems. In reality, this is actually an ability to focus on something other than what is currently demanding our attention. Have you ever heard the saying, "can't see the forest through the trees?" Similar to this idea, if we are only looking at the trees around us, we are unable to see the larger view of the entire forest.

There are two ways to look at situations around us. We need to have the ability to switch back and forth between the two types of views, depending on the needs of the situation. This change may seem like we are distracting ourselves from the problem at hand, but in reality, it is more of a distraction to look at things the wrong way.

The first view is seeing the big picture. You want to see how this particular moment in time fits in the overall scheme of things. The second view is much more specific and focused on a particular detail. Both views are necessary for success, especially in dealing with fear and anxiety.

Turning back to the examples used above, we can see how a simple shift from one view to the other allows us to move forward in life. With the little boy at the gym, he was so focused on the little detail of a scratch on his arm. Nothing else existed except that pain, and he was not about to let go of it. If he had been able to shift his focus to view the bigger picture, he would have seen that he was not in any grave danger from the pain, and that it was a minor setback preventing him from activities he loves to do.

My anxiety at the swing dancing place came from that larger view. I saw everyone and everything at the same time. Pulling that attention into a specific focus allowed me to reset my brain and see the situation by looking at the basics and building upon the pieces I had to work with.

In either case, what seems like a distraction from an initial fear was actually a shift in focus, allowing the problem to be properly dealt with as needed. The situation itself was not avoided, but still dealt with from a different angle. The distractions were used to leverage the focus from one type of view to the other.

Sensory

The most effective way I have found to help change the focus of our view is with sensory stimulation. Our senses are what connect us to the world. So if we change the input coming in through our senses, we are able to adjust the way we view the situation around us. It can completely change what we see going on around us and thus also alter our interpretation of the situation.

In a situation where fear and anxiety start to take control, I use a technique called grounding. This will help reduce the reaction of overwhelm. Look around the room and identify one thing you can see, one thing you can hear, one thing you can touch or feel, one thing you can smell and one thing you can taste. This will pull you from a focused view to a larger view. If you need to go the opposite direction, carry a self-soothe kit that has one item for each sense that you can pull out and focus on.

These soothing kits have been incredibly beneficial for me. Popping a mint into my mouth and focusing on the taste pulls my mind away from the millions of other things my senses try to pick up. If I really need to focus, I try to figure out how I would explain the taste to someone who had never tasted a mint before. I would do the same exercise for any of my other senses as I pull things from my soothe kit. I would attempt to explain the smooth, polished feeling of a stone that I have worn down and created a slight groove in from the repetitive rubbing, or the dance of the glitter as it gently falls to settle in the bottom of a jar. I would focus on the sharp, bright scent of the citrus oil, maybe even place a drop or two on my skin to keep it close. Sound is more difficult for me, so I make sure I have two options. Earplugs to try to block out the sound, but for me this doesn't work as well unless coupled with another sense from my kit, but it might work for another person. The other option that works for me is to focus on the sound of one person talking to me or a close by conversation, or plugging my headphones into my phone and playing a song to focus on.

The point is to focus on one thing and let everything else be swept away. Pay attention to every detail of the sense you have chosen and don't let anything else enter into your brain. Your body will then naturally recover and take care of the rest. Once you are able to calm down, keep what your senses bring in down to a minimum. Focus on your breathing. Focus on one sense at a time and be conscious and intentional as that focus moves from one sense to another without letting it overwhelm you.

Don't open that up even a tiny crack because the pressure will spiral again. A dam can hold back a lot of water, but once there is a single crack in that dam it threatens to, and often does, collapse under the pressure of the water behind it. Your senses will do the same. Once you get everything shut out with laser-intense focus, keep it out and maintain the ground you have gained. Maintenance is far easier than starting over.

Support

I know I mentioned this one already, but the people in your life really are key to helping you overcome fear. I put it here again with the understanding that this is a little different in how it helps you with the during and after phases of scary experiences. I've already discussed how it helps you while going into situations you know will be terrifying and create anxiety or fear.

Whether it's going cliff jumping or making a major life change, the people you have in your life will be the ones who get you through it. Yes, sometimes there are things you will have to do alone, that's just a fact of life. However, knowing that you have people who care for you and support you, even when they aren't right beside you, can make a world of difference. No matter what happens or how bad things get, knowing you are not alone is a complete game-changer. Knowing someone will be there when all is said and done to help you get back on your feet is key to moving forward, whether you do this particular scary activity again or not.

CONCLUSION

I confess, this book was one of the hardest things I've ever done and it terrifies me. Another fear I have is a fairly common one. That I'm not good enough. That I'm not qualified to write a book like this. How can I help others with something I struggle and fight with every day? I am afraid I fight with this a lot. That's probably what makes me the most qualified person to write this book, though. Wouldn't you rather have someone who is right there in the trenches with you than someone telling you what to do from a cushy office chair?

The point is that fear is always going to be a part of your life. Some fears can be overcome, some won't. However, that is never a reason to let it hold you back. Your life is yours to control. Don't let that fear take over the life that is rightfully yours. No matter what the fear is, don't let it affect your decisions. If there is something you want to do, do it! If you don't want to, there is no requirement saying you must. Sometimes you are allowed to walk away from a fear rather than face it. Fears are hard. There is no sense exhausting yourself just trying to constantly face them if it is for something you really have no desire for in the first place.

However, if there is something you want to do, and fear is holding you back, that is a terrible excuse not to pursue it. You have now been given tools to help you face and overcome those fears that keep you from living life on your own terms. It will still be scary, that's not something I can magically take away. Even if I could, I'm not sure that I would.

Facing your fears makes you a stronger person. It is pushing past those fears that make you stand apart from the crowd. And we know my stance on being different and how important that is. Unfortunately, most people aren't willing to face their fears. Kudos to you for being willing and making it through this book. You will go farther in life by facing them and you are well on your way to excellence that most people only dream of achieving...if they weren't so afraid.

Now that you have the right tools and mindset, you are so far ahead of the game. It will certainly take some practice at first, and I'm not saying it's easy by any stretch. But it is possible. Sit down and take a good look at the things you want to do. Then think about the fears that are holding you back. As needed, go back and re-read the sections that are most applicable to help you face and overcome the fears that are standing in your way. Let them make you stronger and more capable.

Build upon the experiences around you, rather than trying to knock them down or run from them. Creating and building may take a lot more time and a lot more hard work, but you will have a lot more to show for it at the end of the day. The life you create, no matter what awkward, tragic or terrifying things life throws at you, is of infinitely more value than the small moment of pain it takes to get there.

My wise friend Richie Norton has said, "don't get discouraged—get creative." There is always a way to get what you want if you are willing to put a bit of thought into it. Most of the fears we face, no matter what they are, aren't really logical. If they are logical, the question becomes, how realistic is it? Outside forces should hold no fear for us. The internal fears are the hard ones to deal with because they can seem so much more real.

These will take the longest to move past. Again, don't get discouraged. Sometimes it will take creativity. Sometimes you won't be able to do it alone. Just know that you don't have to fear what is on the other side. Only good things lie beyond the terrifying smoke barrier in front of you, and only good things are on the other side of it. Life will be different from what you are used to, but again, who said different is a bad thing? And isn't that why you picked up this book in the first place? If being different is a concern for you, please see my book *Awkwardly Strong* to see how important it is to be different. When things seem too hard, please see my book *Tragically Strong*.

You are the only one holding yourself back from all of your wildest dreams. Ironic isn't it? We can want one thing so much and we won't let ourselves have it. Lucky you, now you get to break the chain. This book is a great starting point. Now it's time for you to go take control of your life. Take it back from the fear, the pain and awkwardness that surrounds daily life. Because you deserve better.

ACKNOWLEDGEMENTS

WHILE THIS IS MY FAVORITE PART, it can also be the most difficult. There are so many wonderful people that contribute to my ability to write and publish a book, not to mention my sanity, knowledge and experience. Mom and Dad, thank you for loving me unconditionally, even with all the crazy ideas and chaos I tend to bring with me everywhere I go. Steph, thank you for still acknowledging me as your sister, despite everything, and even more for being my strength. You amaze me. Special thanks to my guardian angels, Travis and Garrett. I may not know how involved you are or be able to see you, but I know my brothers always have my back.

Special thanks should also go to the many, MANY people who have been with me through the scary times, providing love, love, support, space, and anything else I could need. This long list includes all of my sweet grandparents, aunts, uncles and cousins. My family means the world to me, and especially now, and more than ever. Thank you for keeping me sane and taking care of me in my down times. Also thanks to the family by choice who were there for me when things got difficult and I almost gave up on publishing, including the Graham family, Rachael Brandenburg, Beka Reyburn, Kim Kruger, Krystle Carbajal, Keely Lassen and so, so many more. Thank you for your constant love and checking in on me when I needed you most.

I am ever so grateful for Cara Wade and Amber Saffen for figuring out which dictionary to reference when I do a Google search for a word definition (Google pulls definitions from Oxford Dictionary, FYI), and for Cara's several rounds of edits. The cover was done by my friend Megan (Sawyer) Buck, who has recently started her own graphic design company and I am so excited to be a customer of Pixel Perfect Design and Print. I love working with Fran Platt of Eden Graphics on the interior design and formatting of the book. This crew makes my ideas look polished and professional and I am so grateful for them!

This book would not be possible if not for the invaluable guidance and coaching by inspired mentors. I would not be where I am today without Richie Norton, Dr. Benjamin Hardy and Richard Paul Evans. Not only have they each taught me so much, but introduced me to more people who have also continued to teach and provided services for the writing and publishing of my books.

Most importantly, I want to thank and acknowledge YOU. Thank you for reading and supporting me in this journey. It does no good to speak to an empty room. You are providing not only an audience for me to speak to, but encouragement so that I keep going and the funding to do so. You are the best and I'm so grateful for you.

ABOUT THE AUTHOR

PAULA JEAN FERRI is one of the most awkward people you will ever meet. She often screams and makes animal noises in public, sometimes even during work meetings and church services. Having been in multiple awkward situations, she has become a master at the weird and uncomfortable. While always an oddball, the uncontrollable noises started her senior year of high school. At age 24, she was diagnosed with Tourette Syndrome.

Growing up in a small town called Logandale, it wasn't always easy sticking out so much. So upon graduating from high school, she went from small town... to small town, attending college in Ephraim, Utah to attend Snow College before transferring to Laie, Hawaii to finish her undergrad in International Cultural Studies with an emphasis in Communications at Brigham Young University- Hawaii.

She currently resides in Salt Lake City, Utah, where she not only writes but sings, dances, hikes, watches old movies and dreams of the day she can go back to Hawaii and travel the world. Paula Jean is actively involved with her church, attending not only Sunday meetings, but serving in the temple, leading the choir in her congregation and playing sports with the youth. She also loves her visits home to hang out with her family and the three coolest nephews in the world.

For more information on Paula Jean's antics, follow her on Instagram (@jesssqueaks), Facebook (facebook. com/jesssqueaks), or Medium (@jesssqueaks).

Made in the USA
Middletown, DE
24 August 2022